Ojai Valley Slow Cooker Cookbook

vegetarian recipes and tips for your slow cooker

By Randy Graham

© November 23, 2017
Randolph B. Graham
All Rights Reserved

Ojai, California

Front cover photo: Randy Graham

Other books by Randy Graham:
So You've Inherited A Vegetarian...Now What?
Ojai Valley Gluten-Free Cookbook
Ojai Valley Vegetarian Cookbook
Ojai Valley Vegan Cookbook
Ojai Valley Blog Book

Many thanks to my friends for reviewing my draft and providing input prior to submitting this book for publication: Carol Miller, Lol Sorensen, Lynn Gaede, Heather Rowe, Marcia Morris, Stacy Ann Allison, Rae Erickson Hanstad, Pat Faye, Lori Hamor, Donna Lloyd, Margaret Marapao, Frances Lunny, Steve Weeks, Katrina Sexton, Cathy and Tom Okerlund, and Jennifer Totaro.

Table of Contents

Introduction

History of the Slow Cooker

Slow Cooker Safety

Quicker/Nutritious Recipes
1. Savory Vegetarian Stew *VEGAN*
2. Hearty Chili Bean Soup *VEGAN*
3. Beefless Stew with Sofrito *VEGAN*
4. Minestrone Soup *VEGAN*
5. Taste of Morocco *VEGAN*
6. Spinach, Bean, and Sausage Soup
7. Chili Verde *VEGAN*
8. Hearty Sorghum Soup
9. Curried Vegetable and Chickpea Stew *VEGAN*
10. Boeufless Bourguignon *VEGAN*
11. Alphabet Soup
12. Butternut Squash Stew *VEGAN*
13. Chik'n Tikka Masala *VEGAN*
14. Lentil Stew with Sausage
15. Mulligatawny Soup *VEGAN*
16. Risotto with Barley
17. Southwest Vegetarian Stew
18. Navy Bean Soup *VEGAN*
19. Quinoa and Chik'n Enchilada Casserole

Not Necessarily Nutritious (but fun)
20. Apple Butter *VEGAN*
21. Bananas Foster
22. Dulce de Leche

Index of Recipes by Title

Index of Ingredients by Recipe

About the Author

Introduction

Imagine opening the front door on a cold winter evening and being greeted by the inviting smells of homemade soup or stew wafting from a slow cooker. It is a mom's dream come true. But winter is not the only time a slow cooker is useful. In the summer, using this small countertop appliance can avoid using a hot stove. And it takes less electricity to use a slow cooker than a stove.

This cookbook is written for my single mom friends and for all of my friends who have expressed a need to eat nutritiously but don't have the time to plan, prep, and cook after a long day of work. It boasts 19 tried-and-true slow cooker double recipes. *Double, you ask? What do you mean by double?*

Each of the first 19 recipes contains both quicker and nutritious versions of the same recipe. The Chili Verde recipe, for example, includes a quicker version with eight ingredients that you toss into the slow cooker, stir once, cover, and return hours later to a tasty dinner. It takes five minutes or less to prep. The more nutritious version takes about 45 minutes to prep and, instead of using canned or frozen ingredients, calls for fresh ingredients such as Poblano and jalapeño peppers, onions, garlic, cilantro, and tomatillos.

All quick versions can be prepped and placed into the slow cooker in 10 minutes or less. Turn on the slow cooker and forget about it. The nutritious versions take anywhere from 20 to 60 minutes to prepare and, because they use fresh ingredients, are more nutritious.

Both recipe versions are tasty and vegetarian. Both will put a smile on your face.

In addition to the above, there are three dessert recipes. Although not necessarily as quick or nutritious as the original 19, they are easy and fun. For example who would think to make slow cooker apple butter that lasts all week long in the refrigerator? And Bananas Foster. Making this classic dessert is super easy and tastes as good if not better than that made on the hot stove top. Don't forget to try Dulce de Leche. Make it as you have time and use for cookies, as a topping for ice cream, or just as a tasty spoonful-by-spoonful treat after dinner.

Here's what I recommend to maximize your time and effort:

- Choose one day of the week to prepare and serve a slow cooker meal. You might, for example, choose Monday. Maybe even call it meatless Monday.

- Choose a recipe from this cookbook for Meatless Monday one week ahead of time.

- Shop for the ingredients sometime during the week before so that when you prep the meal, everything will be available to you. Who wants to go to the store at the last minute?

- On the Sunday night before preparing the recipe, put all non-perishable ingredients out on the kitchen counter so they are easily accessible the next morning. If going with the quicker versions there is little if any need for prep.

- Get up 15 to 30 minutes earlier than usual on Monday morning, open cans if necessary, measure out all ingredients and add to slow cooker. Then set it to cook, and you can continue with the rest of your morning activities knowing dinner is taken care of.

Every effort has been taken to create recipes that are distinctly different from one another, and that will easily serve four adults. After making one or two recipes you and your family will be chanting my mantra, "Eat well. Eat local. Eat fresh!"

The Slow Cooker and Other Devices

When I first pitched the idea for this cookbook I was asked, *what is a slow cooker and how does it differ from a Crock-Pot?*

My reply was that a slow cooker is an appliance that sits on your countertop and plugs into an electrical outlet. Crock-Pot is a brand name for a slow cooker that was effectively marketed in the early '70s by Rival Manufacturing. Both Rival's Crock-Pot and today's slow cooker knockoffs have three basic components: a pot (usually ceramic), a lid (usually glass), and an electric heating element. Otherwise, the two are very similar in that they both use a low, moist heat to cook food evenly over a long period of time (usually 3 to 8 hours).

The history of Rival's original Crock Pot is worth mentioning. According to the website cnet.com:

> *On May 21, 1936, Irving Naxon, a prolific inventor, applied for a patent for a cooking device that would not only be portable, but would provide solutions for many complaints issued about previous models, namely uneven heating. It was to be an integrated appliance, with the cooking vessel (the crock) housed inside a casing that also contained the heating element, allowing the heat to distribute more evenly.*
>
> *Naxon received the patent for this appliance in January 1940, but he credits his inspiration*

to his grandmother (nee Nachumsohn) who told him about a dish she made growing up in Lithuania--scholent-- and how she would cook it after hours at a local bakery, using the fading heat of the bakery's oven to cook the dish overnight. By integrating the crock inside of the heating unit, Naxon captured that "low and slow" cooking process and made it accessible to the mid-20th-century cook.

Naxon brought his device, the Naxon Beanery, to market in the 1950's. In 1970, the Rival Manufacturing acquired Naxon and, in 1972, rebranded the Beanery as the Crock-Pot. The appliance retailed for about $25, a price that has held steady, even with inflation. You can buy more expensive slow-cookers now, but you can also go to your local superstore and, depending on the brand or model, buy a slow cooker for $25, if not less. In its debut, the Crock-Pot came in such classic 1970s colors as copper, harvest gold, and avocado, and it also included its own Crock-Pot specific cookbook.

I had the copper model and used it for many years with its single control knob (off/low/high). Today's slow cookers offer many convenient features such as programmable heat and time settings. Some even come with external temperature probes. Other types of countertop cooking appliances include stove top pressure cookers, electric pressure cookers, and multicookers.

Stove top pressure cookers use steam in a sealed vessel, permitting the steam to escape below a preset pressure. Because the boiling point of water increases as the pressure increases, the pressure built up inside the cooker allows the liquid in the cooking pot to rise to a higher temperature before boiling and food cook more quickly than conventional methods. Some units cook meals up to 70% faster.

Electric pressure cookers are similar to conventional pressure cookers but with a built-in microprocessor unit that monitors and regulates the cooking process for you. Because the heating process is controlled by the microprocessor (based on readings from pressure and temperature sensors), it is a very efficient with a safe closed-loop controlled cooking system.

Multicookers are an amazing counter top combination of pressure cooker and slow cooker. They boast the ability to cook, among other things, regular slow cooker recipes, steamed rice, and bread. They can also act like an oven, a range top, and a fryer with variable heat settings from 110 to 450 degrees Fahrenheit.

Slow Cooker Safety

The thought of cooking food slowly for up to eight hours on your countertop might trigger fears of unsafe bacteria. So, is the food that's been simmering all day long on your kitchen counter safe to feed your family?

The short answer is yes. The long answer is that it is hotter in the slow cooker than you might think. The combination of heat and lengthy cooking times keeps foods between 170 degrees (low setting) and 280 degrees (high setting). That's hot enough to destroy bad bacteria.

Here are some tips for safely preparing and cooking:

- Read and follow the instructions that come with your slow cooker before cooking your first meal.

- Make sure your slow cooker, utensils, and work area are clean and sanitized. Be sure to wash your hands before beginning prep and occasionally while preparing food.

- Keep perishable foods refrigerated until you need them. If you plan to prep ahead of time, keep prepped foods in the refrigerator until ready to put in the slow cooker. Your slow cooker might take a while to reach 165 degrees, which is widely regarded as the temperature at which most illness-causing bacteria are killed. Keeping ingredients in the fridge helps deny bacteria a chance to multiply wildly in those critical first hours of cooking.

- Most slow cookers heat from the sides instead of the bottom as in stove-top cooking. For best results, the slow cooker should be at least half full of ingredients: add the solid ingredients first, then cover with water and stock or broth as directed in the recipe.

- Avoid removing the lid until the end of cooking. It takes approximately 20 minutes to recover lost heat so keep the lid firmly in place, removing it only to check for doneness.

- Don't reheat leftovers in the slow cooker. Leftovers should be stored in shallow, covered containers and refrigerated within two hours.

Quicker/Nutritious Recipes

[Beefless Stew with Sofrito #3]

1. Savory Vegetarian Stew (quicker) *VEGAN*

The secret to this recipe is slow cooking on low heat overnight. The organic style tofu stays firm and soaks up the savory flavors of the onion, garlic, rosemary, basil, and bay leaf. I like to use the leaf of the California bay tree (sometimes referred to as the California laurel) because of its strong flavor.

Ingredients:
1 pound organic style tofu (extra firm)
¼ teaspoon ground cloves
1 tablespoon onion powder
½ teaspoon corn starch
2 teaspoons garlic powder
1 bay leaf
¼ teaspoon dried basil
¼ teaspoon dried sage
2-inch slice of orange rind
½ teaspoon sugar
15-ounce can whole new potatoes –cut in half (such as Del Monte)
12 baby or petite cut carrots (such as Bolthouse Farms)
1 cup white wine
3 cups vegetable broth
Salt to taste

Directions:
Plug in and set slow cooker to low.

Prepare tofu for cooking by cutting into 1-inch cubes and placing them in the slow cooker. Add all other ingredients except salt. Stir, cover and cook for 7 hours. Taste and add salt if needed. Serve while still hot!

Prepare in the morning, and it will be done by dinner time. Prepare before going to bed, and it will be done in the morning for reheating any time during the day or night. Serve warm with fresh baguette (for dipping in stew).

Makes a whole bunch of stew. If you have any leftover, put it in a baggie and place it in the freezer for next week.

1. Savory Vegetarian Stew (nutritious) *VEGAN*

Ingredients:
1 pound organic style tofu (extra firm)
4 whole cloves
1 large white or yellow onion (peeled and cut into quarters)
½ teaspoon corn starch
4 cloves garlic (minced)
1 bay leaf
¼ teaspoon dried basil
¼ teaspoon dried sage
2-inch slice of orange rind
½ teaspoon turbinado sugar
1 large potato (cut into 1½ inch cubes)
4 to 6 fresh carrots (cut into thirds –scrubbed but not peeled)
1 cup white wine
3 cups vegetable broth
Salt to taste

Directions:
Plug in and set slow cooker to low.

To prepare tofu, cut it into 1-inch thick slices. Place a layer of 4 to 5 paper towels on a flat surface and lay tofu on towels. Place another layer of 4 to 5 towels over the tofu. Lay a cutting board over the tofu and place a weight on top of the. This will absorb excess water from the tofu allowing the tofu to soak up the broth while cooking. The tofu will be ready in approximately 20 minutes. Prepare tofu for cooking by cutting into 1-inch cubes.

Place tofu in the slow cooker. Stick cloves into onion quarters and add to pot. Add the balance of the ingredients (except salt) to the pot. Stir, cover and cook for 7 hours. Taste and add salt if needed. Serve while still hot!

Prepare in the morning, and it will be done by dinner time. Prepare before going to bed, and it will be done in the morning for reheating any time during the day or night. Serve warm with fresh baguette (for dipping in stew).

This recipe makes a whole bunch of stew. If you have any left over, freeze it for next week.

2. Hearty Chili Bean Soup (quicker) *VEGAN*

I first developed this as a chili for the many chili cook-off events in which I've participated. Our son, Robert, helped serve at the cook-offs. Although the chili never won any awards, it was unique, interesting, and a welcome addition to the *meaty* chili dishes.

One rainy winter afternoon, I wanted hot soup but also had a hankering for chili beans. I dusted off my old Vegetarian Chili Beans recipe and tweaked it into a superb, hearty soup. This vegan recipe uses a slow cooker to maximize flavor.

Get it started at noontime and it will be ready for dinner. Serve with fresh, hot cornbread, and a garden salad for a completely nutritious and delicious meal.

Ingredients:
2 15-ounce cans pinto beans (do not drain)
2½ cups water
2 vegetable bouillon cubes
2 tablespoons vegetable oil
1 tablespoon onion powder
1 teaspoon garlic powder
12 baby or petite cut carrots (such as Bolthouse Farms)
5 tablespoons dried bell pepper flakes (such as Cain's)
15-ounce can new potatoes (drained)
28-ounce can diced tomatoes (do not drain)
1 teaspoon ground cumin

1 teaspoon dried basil
¼ teaspoon dried oregano
2 teaspoons lime juice
1 heaping tablespoon chili powder
1 to 3 teaspoons hot sauce (depending on how hot you like it)
1 teaspoon salt
¼ teaspoon pepper

Directions:
Plug in and set slow cooker to high.

Add all ingredients to slow cooker except for salt and pepper. Cover and cook for 4 hours. Add salt and pepper to taste just and stir before serving.

2. Heart Chili Bean Soup (nutritious) *VEGAN*

Ingredients:
2 tablespoons extra virgin olive oil
1 large onion (chopped)
3 to 4 cloves garlic (crushed)
1 large bell pepper (chopped)
1 carrot (unpeeled –scrubbed and diced)
1 large red potato (unpeeled and diced)
28-ounce can organic diced fire roasted tomatoes (do not drain)
2 jalapeno peppers (seeded and diced)
2 15-ounce cans organic pinto beans (do not drain)
2½ cups water
2 tablespoons Better Than Bouillon Vegetable Base
1 teaspoon ground cumin
3 teaspoons fresh basil (chopped)
¼ teaspoon dried oregano
2 teaspoons fresh lime juice
1 heaping tablespoon chili powder
1 to 3 teaspoons Tabasco Sauce (depending on how hot you like it)
1 teaspoon salt
Fresh ground black pepper (to taste)

Directions:
Plug in and set slow cooker to high.

Add oil, onions, and garlic to a large skillet and sauté over medium heat for about 5 minutes. Add bell pepper, carrot, potato, tomatoes (including liquid) and jalapeno peppers. Deglaze pan and cook for another 5 minutes.

Add beans (including liquid) and water to slow cooker. Add onion mixture and next seven ingredients (bouillon to Tabasco Sauce) to slow cooker. Cover and cook for 4 hours. Add salt and pepper and stir before serving.

3. Beefless Stew with Sofrito (quicker) *VEGAN*

Aromatic and savory, sofrito is a condiment, sauce, and a base for many Caribbean dishes from countries such as Puerto Rico, Dominican Republic, and Cuba. In short, it is versatile. And it is flavorful. Super flavorful.

Sofrito has its origins in Spanish cuisine and typically consists of onions sautéed in oil with ingredients like garlic, hot and/or sweet peppers, tomatoes, and herbs such as cilantro, culantro, and oregano. Some sofritos are red, others are green, some are chunky, and others puréed.

My version is pureed and vegetarian. I substitute Gardein Beefless Tips for beef. It is tasty, easy to use, and most of all has the texture necessary for a slow cooker recipe.

Ingredients:
2 packages Gardein Beefless Tips
1/2 cup ready chopped onions (such as Birds Eye)
½ teaspoon garlic powder
15-ounce can new potatoes (drained)
15-ounce can diced tomatoes
1/2 cup pitted green olives (such as Lindsay Naturals)
½ teaspoon black pepper
12 ounces Sofrito (such as Goya)
¼ cup water

Directions:
Plug in and set slow cooker to low.

Add all ingredients to slow cooker. Stir, cover, and cook for 3½ hours. Before serving, taste and adjust for salt (if necessary). Serve with a side of rice and fresh garden salad.

Note: This recipe makes about 5 cups of stew. It can easily be doubled if you need more!

3. Beefless Stew with Sofrito (nutritious) *VEGAN*

Stew Ingredients:
1/2 cup yellow onion (diced)
2 cloves garlic (minced)
2 packages Gardein Beefless Tips
2 cups red potatoes (not peeled, cut into 1-inch cubes)
15-ounce can diced tomatoes
½ cup pitted green olives (such as Lindsay Naturals)
½ teaspoon salt
½ teaspoon fresh ground black pepper
1½ cups Sofrito (make ahead - see below*)
¼ cup water

Stew Directions:
Plug in and set slow cooker to low.

Heat a large skillet over medium heat. Sauté onion and garlic until softened, about 5 minutes. Add onions/garlic to slow cooker. Stir in balance of ingredients (Gardein Beefless thru water).

Cook for 4 hours. Before serving, taste and adjust for salt (if necessary). Serve with a side of rice and fresh garden salad.

Note: This recipe makes about 5 cups of stew. It can easily be doubled if you need more!

* Sofrito Ingredients:
2 medium yellow onions (cut 1-inch chunks)
4 cubanelle peppers (seeded, cut 1-inch chunks)

18 medium cloves garlic (peeled)
1 large bunch of cilantro (washed and chopped)
4 leaves of culantro
4 ripe plum tomatoes (cored, cut 1-inch chunks)
2 medium red bell peppers (seeded, cut 1-inch chunks)
Salt to taste

Sofrito Directions:
Heat oil in a skillet over medium heat. Add onions and cubanelle peppers and sauté until onions are soft. Place onions and cubanelle peppers in the bowl of a 6-cup food processor fitted with a steel blade. Pulse until very coarsely chopped.

4. Minestrone Soup (quicker) *VEGAN*

Minestrone is a thick soup containing vegetables and pasta. The word originated from the Italian language word *minestrare, which means* to serve. According to the Princeton.edu website:

> *Some of the earliest origins of minestrone soup pre-date the expansion of the Latin tribes of Rome into what became the Roman Republic and later Roman Empire, when the local diet was "vegetarian by necessity" and consisted mostly of vegetables, such as onions, lentils, cabbage, garlic, fava beans, mushrooms, carrots, asparagus and turnips.*

> *It wasn't until the 2nd century B.C., when Rome had conquered Italy and monopolized the commercial and road networks, that a huge diversity of products flooded the capital and began to change their diet, and by association, the diet of Italy most notably with the more frequent inclusion of meats, including as a stock for soups.*

This vegan recipe makes enough hearty soup to feed four hungry people. Best of all, it is easy to make, and the slow cooker brings out the best in both the vegetables and the herbs. Make it first thing in the morning and reheat for dinner.

Ingredients:
4 cups vegetable broth
1½ cups water
2 vegetable bouillon cubes
15-ounce can diced tomatoes
8 baby or petite cut carrots (such as Bolthouse Farms)
¼ cup dried celery flakes (such as McCormick)
1 tablespoon onion powder
1 teaspoon dried parsley
2 teaspoons dried basil
1 teaspoon dried oregano
½ teaspoon dried thyme
2 bay leaves
1 teaspoon garlic powder
15-ounce can dark red kidney beans (drained and rinsed)
15-ounce can cannellini beans (drained and rinsed)
15-ounce can zucchini with tomato sauce
15-ounce can Italian green beans (drained)
1 1/3 cups uncooked orecchiette pasta
10 ounces frozen spinach leaves –thawed (such as Birds Eye)
Salt and freshly ground black pepper to taste

Directions:
Plug in and set slow cooker to high.

Add first fifteen ingredients (vegetable broth thru cannellini beans) to slow cooker. Cover and cook for 3 hours.

Turn heat to low. Add zucchini, green beans, and pasta and cook for an additional 60 minutes. Check seasoning and if it needs more salt and pepper, season to taste. Add spinach and cook for several minutes more or until spinach is heated through. Look for and remove the bay leaves before serving.

Serve with fresh, crusty French bread.

4. Minestrone Soup (nutritious) *VEGAN*

Ingredients:
4 cups vegetable broth
2 teaspoons Better Than Bouillon Vegetable Base
1½ cups water
2 15-ounce cans diced tomatoes
3 stalks celery (diced)
2 large carrots (diced)
1 small yellow onion (diced)
1 tablespoon fresh parsley (chopped)
2 tablespoons fresh basil leaves
1 tablespoon fresh oregano
1 teaspoon fresh thyme
1 teaspoon fresh rosemary (chopped)
4 cloves garlic (minced)
2 bay leaves
1 small zucchini (diced)
1 1/3 cups uncooked orecchiette pasta
15-ounce can dark red kidney beans (drained and rinsed)
15-ounce can cannellini beans (drained and rinsed)
15-ounce can Italian green beans (drained)
12 ounces fresh baby spinach
Salt and freshly ground black pepper to taste

Directions:
Plug in and set slow cooker to high.

Add first fourteen ingredients (vegetable broth thru bay leaves) to slow cooker. Cover and cook on high for 3 hours.

Turn heat to low. Add zucchini, pasta, kidney beans and cannellini beans and cook for an additional 60 minutes. Stir in green beans and spinach and cook for several minutes more or until green beans are heated through. Check seasoning and if it needs more salt and pepper, season to taste. Look for and remove the bay leaves before serving.

Serve with fresh, crusty French bread.

5. Taste of Morocco (quicker) *VEGAN*

This vegan dish has an excellent combination of flavors. Whether enjoyed for lunch or dinner it is a complete meal. Serve it with fresh, warm pita bread or naan. For a real treat, turn the lights down low, put on the ZBS audio production *Moon Over Morocco*[*] and imagine you are in the heart of Casablanca as you enjoy this unusual dish from North Africa.

Ingredients:
1 tablespoon olive oil
1 tablespoon onion powder
12 baby or petite cut carrots (such as Bolthouse Farms)
¼ teaspoon garlic powder
1 pound organic extra firm tofu (cut into 1-inch cubes)
¼ teaspoon black pepper
1 tablespoon paprika
1 teaspoon cumin
1 teaspoon cinnamon
15-ounce can chickpeas
1/3 cup dried apricots (chopped)
¼ cup raisins
¼ cup fresh cilantro (chopped)
¼ cup fresh mint (chopped)
16 ounces vegetable broth
Salt to taste

Directions:
Plug in and set slow cooker to high.

Add all ingredients to the slow cooker (except salt). Cover and cook for 3½ hours. Before serving, taste and adjust salt to taste.

ZBS is a not-for-profit arts organization producing radio/audio stories since 1970. Moon over Morocco is one of our favorite stories with background sounds recorded by author M. Fulton while traveling around that country. See www.zbs.org for more information.

5. Taste of Morocco (nutritious) *VEGAN*

Ingredients:
1 tablespoon olive oil
1 large yellow onion (chopped)
3 carrots (cleaned & chopped —no need to peel)
1 clove garlic (minced)
1 pound organic extra firm tofu (cut into 1-inch cubes)
¼ teaspoon fresh ground pepper
1 tablespoon paprika
1 teaspoon cumin
1 teaspoon cinnamon
16 ounces organic vegetable broth
1 teaspoon Better Than Bouillon Vegetable Base
15-ounce can chickpeas
1/3 cup dried apricots (chopped)
¼ cup raisins
¼ cup fresh cilantro (chopped)
¼ cup fresh mint (chopped)
Salt to taste

Directions:
Plug in and set slow cooker to high.

In a 3-quart sauté pan bring oil to medium heat. Add onion, carrots, garlic, and tofu. Sauté over medium-high heat for about 3 minutes. Add balance of ingredients (except salt) and cook, stirring frequently for another 4-5 minutes.

Add the contents of the sauté pan to the slow cooker, cover, and cook for 3½ hours. Before serving, taste and adjust salt to taste.

6. Spinach, Bean, and Sausage Soup (quicker)

I like this recipe because it includes a "meaty" vegetarian sausage. I know. An oxymoron. A contradiction in terms. Perhaps...but this sausage is tasty and nutritious!

One sausage, for example, contains 140 total calories of which only 60 are from fat* and boasts 13 grams of protein. These sausages are made with, among other ingredients, soy proteins, wheat gluten, and egg whites and are cholesterol free. They hold up well in the slow cooker without breaking down; that is, they still have that "sausage" bite and texture after cooking on high for four hours.

With the addition of Cannellini beans, carrots, and spinach, this is a nutritionally balanced meal that is sure to satisfy you and your family.

Ingredients:
1 tablespoon extra-virgin olive oil
2 15-ounce cans Cannellini beans (drained and rinsed)
1 package Lightlife Smart Sausages Italian Style (cut into ½-inch pieces)
¾ teaspoon garlic powder
1 cup frozen diced onions (such as Birds Eye)
1/3 cup celery flakes
½ teaspoon dried oregano
2 bay leaves
4 cups vegetable broth
2 cups water

10 ounces frozen spinach leaves –defrosted (such as Birds Eye)
Salt and freshly ground black pepper to taste

Directions:
Plug in and set slow cooker to high.

Place first 10 ingredients (olive oil thru water) in slow cooker. Cover and cook for 4 hours. Before serving, remove bay leaves and add spinach. Stir to combine. Cook, uncovered, on high heat for approximately 15 minutes or until spinach is wilted. Add salt and pepper to taste.

For a complete meal, serve with fresh French bread or a baguette.

By comparison, one Johnsonville mild Italian meat sausage contains 260 total calories of which 190 are from fat.

6. Spinach, Bean, and Sausage Soup (nutritious)

Ingredients:
1 tablespoon extra-virgin olive oil
1 package Lightlife Smart Sausages Italian Style (cut into ½-inch pieces)
3 cloves garlic (minced)
1 onion (diced)
3 stalks celery (diced)
2 15-ounce cans Cannellini beans (drained and rinsed)
1/2 teaspoon dried oregano
2 bay leaves
4 cups vegetable broth
2 cups water
3 cups baby spinach leaves
Salt and freshly ground black pepper to taste

Directions:
Plug in and set slow cooker to high.

Heat olive oil in a large skillet over medium-high heat. Add sausage, and cook, stirring frequently, until lightly browned, about 3-4 minutes.

Place sausage, garlic, onion, celery, beans, oregano, and bay leaves into slow cooker. Add broth and water and stir until well combined. Cover and cook for 4 hours. Stir in spinach and cook for another 15 minutes or until wilted. Add salt and pepper to taste. Remove bay leaves before serving. For a complete meal, serve with fresh French bread or a baguette.

7. Chili Verde (quicker) *VEGAN*

There is nothing better than a good bowl of Chili Verde for warming your belly this winter. What is the difference between chili and Chili Verde? The short answer is that chili came first followed by Chili Verde.

A chile is a vegetable (well...technically a fruit). Chile can be made into chili, but not vice versa. "Chili" is a stew made with meat and beans although Texans would challenge the beans as an ingredient. As my brother, who lives in San Antonio might say, "If you know beans about chili, you know that chili has no beans." Chili, not surprisingly, is the official state food of Texas and is commonly referred to as a "bowl of red".

"Verde" is the Spanish language word for green. Chili Verde is a stew made of sauce with green chiles (such as Poblano, jalapeño, and serrano), tomatillos, onions, and garlic. Pork or beef chunks are added to this sauce.

It is said that Canary Islanders, transplanted in the early 1700s to San Antonio, Texas, used local chile peppers, wild onions, garlic, and other spices to concoct a pungent meat stew which came to be called chili. The National Chili Day website (yes, there is a national chili day) says that chili was widely recognized by the late 1800s.

In the 1880s, a market in San Antonio started setting up chili stands from which chili or bowls o'red, as it was called, were sold by women who were called "chili queens." A bowl o'red cost diners such as writer O. Henry and democratic presidential hopeful William Jennings Bryan ten cents and included bread and a glass of water. The fame of chili con carne began to spread and the dish soon became a major tourist attraction. It was featured at the World's Fair in Chicago in 1893 at the San Antonio Chili Stand.

By the 20th-century chili joints had made their debut in Texas and became familiar all over the west by the roaring '20s. In fact, by the end of that decade, there was hardly a town that didn't have a chili parlor, which was often no more than a shed or a room with a counter and some stools. It's been said that chili joints meant the difference between starvation and staying alive during the Great Depression since chili was cheap and crackers were free.

Family-run chili joints, also known as chili parlors, spread across Texas. Somewhere about this same time green chiles and tomatillos found their way into Texas chili. Before you could say Bob's your uncle, a bowl of red turned green. Recipes for Chili Verde spread throughout the southwest and into Mexico.

As you might expect, recipes for this green stew vary according to regional and cultural differences. In the state of Chihuahua, Mexico, for example, the sauce for Chili Verde consists of roasted chilaca peppers and very little if any tomatillos. If you go further south, Chili Verde consists of lots of tomatillos and bits of jalapeno peppers which are hotter than chilacas.

In New Mexico, folks will tell you their version of Chili Verde is not Mexican or Texan. *It is*, they might say, *its own special animal*. The New Mexico version takes advantage of local Hatch Valley green chile peppers (roasted of course). The Hatch pepper is to Chili Verde in New Mexico as no-beans chili is to chili in Texas. You can use whatever chiles you prefer if you make Chili Verde in New Mexico, but If it doesn't have green Hatch peppers, it's not Chili Verde.

In California, we find many versions of Chili Verde on the menus in Mexican restaurants, cafes, and taquerias. My version is made overnight in a slow cooker. Because I am a vegetarian chef, my recipe calls for Quorn Vegan Chik'n Tenders as opposed to pork or beef, and as you might expect, it would not be recognized as Chili Verde outside of California. By cooking for a few hours in a slow cooker, the ingredients come together to make a sauce that is outstanding.

What, then, is the essence of good Chili Verde? To paraphrase the tagline from the 1991 movie "Fried Green Tomatoes," *the essence is in the sauce!*

Ingredients:
1 package Quorn Vegan Chik'n Tenders
10-ounce can green enchilada sauce (such as Old El Paso)

½ cup water
14-ounce can chopped tomatoes (with liquid)
1½ teaspoons ground cumin
2 teaspoons chili powder
½ teaspoon garlic powder
Salt and fresh ground black pepper to taste
1 cup ready chopped onions (such as Birds Eye –for garnish)
Fresh cilantro (chopped for garnish)

Directions:
Plug in and set slow cooker to high.

Add first eight ingredients (Quorn through salt and pepper) to slow cooker. Stir well to combine. Cover and cook for 3 hours. Spoon into individual bowls and top with diced onions and fresh cilantro. Serve with warm tortillas and/or with rice and beans on the side.

7. Chili Verde (nutritious) VEGAN

Ingredients:
9 Poblano chiles
2 jalapeño chiles
8 large tomatillos (husks removed and cut in quarters)
1 tablespoon extra-virgin olive oil
1 medium yellow onion (diced)
6 cloves garlic (minced)
1 cup chopped cilantro (divided)
½ teaspoon salt
1 teaspoon cracked black pepper
3½ cups vegetable broth
1 tablespoon ground cumin
1 tablespoon dried Mexican oregano
¼ teaspoon ground allspice
4 teaspoons masa harina (thickener)
1 package Quorn Vegan Chik'n Tenders
1 tablespoon freshly squeezed lime juice
Sour cream (for garnish)
Additional chopped cilantro (for garnish)
Fresh lime wedges (served on the side)

Directions:
Plug in and set slow cooker to high.

Roast Poblano and jalapeño chiles by placing them under the broiler of the oven. Roast for about 20 minutes total time, turning every 4 or 5 minutes until deeply charred on all surfaces.

Remove chiles from oven and place in a large baggie. Seal and let steam for 15 minutes. Peel away the skins using your hands (if still too hot, wait another 5 minutes). Discard seeds and stems, and chop chiles coarsely.

Place chiles, the tomatillos, olive oil, onion, garlic, and ½ cup of the cilantro in a food processor. Pulse until mixture is pureed. Season to taste with cracked pepper.

Place pureed mixture in slow cooker along with the broth, cumin, oregano, allspice, masa harina, Quorn and the other ½ cup chopped cilantro. Stir to combine, cover, and cook for 3 hours.

Add lime juice and stir to combine. Spoon Chili Verde into individual bowls, and top with a dollop of sour cream and a sprinkling of fresh cilantro. Serve with a side of warm tortillas and fresh lime wedges. Add a side of rice for a complete meal.

8. Hearty Sorghum Soup (quicker)

Sorghum is a gluten-free grain that has a chewy texture similar to Israeli couscous. Some sources say it was cultivated for 3,000 years and more. This gluten-free soup is as tasty as it is easy to prepare. If you are looking for a good bowl of "hearty," this is the soup for you. Give it a try. You and your family will be glad you did.

Ingredients:
1½ tablespoons olive oil
1 cup chopped onions
1 pound fresh mushrooms
3 cloves garlic (minced)
¼ teaspoon dried thyme
3/4 cup uncooked sorghum grain
2 stalks celery (sliced)
2 large carrots (sliced)
½ bay leaf
6 cups vegetable broth
Salt and fresh ground black pepper to taste
Romano cheese (grated for garnish)

Directions:
Plug in and set slow cooker to high.

Heat olive oil in a sauce pan over medium-high heat and sauté onions for 5 minutes. Clean, remove stems and cut mushrooms into quarters. Add mushrooms, garlic, thyme, and sorghum to the pan. Stir to combine and cook for another 4 minutes stirring once every minute or so.

Pour mushroom mixture into slow cooker. Add the celery, carrots, bay leaf, and broth. Cover and cook for 4 hours.

Season with salt and pepper to taste. Remove bay leaf and spoon soup into individual bowls. Grate Romano cheese on top and serve with a fresh baguette or two!

8. Hearty Sorghum Soup (nutritious)

Ingredients:
1½ tablespoons olive oil
1 cup chopped onions
1 pound fresh mushrooms
3 cloves garlic (minced)
¼ teaspoon dried thyme
3/4 cup uncooked sorghum grain
2 stalks celery (sliced)
2 large carrots (sliced)
½ bay leaf
6 cups vegetable broth
Salt and fresh ground black pepper to taste
Romano cheese (grated for garnish)

Directions:
Plug in and set slow cooker to high.

Heat olive oil in a sauce pan over medium-high heat and sauté onions for 5 minutes. Clean, remove stems and cut mushrooms into quarters. Add mushrooms, garlic, thyme, and sorghum to the pan. Stir to combine and cook for another 4 minutes stirring once every minute or so.

Pour mushroom mixture into slow cooker. Add the celery, carrots, bay leaf, and broth. Cover and cook for 4 hours.

Season with salt and pepper to taste. Remove bay leaf and spoon soup into individual bowls. Grate Romano cheese on top and serve with a fresh baguette or two!

9. Curried Vegetable and Chickpea Stew (quicker) *VEGAN*

Curry refers to a number of saucy dishes flavored with curry powder or curry paste. Curry is made of a blend of various spices and herbs including, but not limited to, cloves, cardamom, ginger, nutmeg, fennel, caraway, ajowan seeds, dried basil, mustard seeds, mace, poppy seeds, sesame seeds, saffron or cinnamon.

But it's not just the blend of spices that make my curry. It is also the green peppers, cauliflower, tomatoes (OK...the seeds are on the inside, so they are technically a fruit), spinach and potatoes. Healthy and tasty. Can't get much better than that!

This curry is quick and easy to make. If you are like me, you'll take your time to put love and good intentions into this dish. It's even better that way.

Ingredients:
1 teaspoon extra-virgin olive oil
1 cup ready chopped onions (such as Birds Eye)
15 ounces Simply Potatoes (diced)
1 tablespoon salt
1 tablespoon curry powder
Pinch of cayenne pepper
1 tablespoon brown sugar
1 teaspoon ground ginger
¾ teaspoon garlic powder
2½ cups vegetable broth
2 15-ounce cans chickpeas (drained)
16 ounces frozen chopped green peppers

14 ounce bag frozen cauliflower florets (such as Birds Eye)
28-ounce can diced tomatoes (with liquid)
¼ teaspoon fresh ground black pepper
10 ounces fresh baby spinach
1 cup coconut milk

Directions:
Plug in and set slow cooker to high.

Add first 15 ingredients (olive oil thru black pepper) to the slow cooker. Stir to combine, cover, and cook for 3½ hours. Stir in the spinach and coconut milk. Cover with lid for a few more minutes to allow the spinach to get warm (wilted). Serve over rice for a complete meal.

9. Curried Vegetable and Chickpea Stew (nutritious) *VEGAN*

Ingredients:
1 teaspoon extra-virgin olive oil
1 large onion (diced)
2 medium red potatoes (not peeled but diced)
1 tablespoon curry powder
Pinch of cayenne pepper
3 cloves (minced)
1 tablespoon brown sugar
1 tablespoon fresh ginger (grated)
2½ cups vegetable broth (divided)
2 15-ounce cans chickpeas (drained)
1 green bell pepper (diced)
1 red bell pepper (diced)
1 medium head fresh cauliflower (florets only)
28-ounce can diced tomatoes (with liquid)
1 tablespoon salt
¼ teaspoon fresh ground black pepper
10 ounces fresh baby spinach
1 cup coconut milk

Directions:
Plug in and set slow cooker to high.

Heat the oil in a skillet over medium heat. Sauté the onion until translucent, about 5 minutes. Add the potatoes and sauté for another 4 to 5 minutes. Stir in the curry, cayenne, garlic, brown sugar, and ginger. Cook until fragrant, about 30 seconds.

Pour in ½ cup of broth and scrape up any toasty bits from the bottom of the pan. Transfer this onion-potato mixture into the slow cooker. Add the rest of the broth, chickpeas, bell pepper, cauliflower, tomatoes, salt, and pepper. Stir to combine, cover, and cook for 4 hours.

Stir in the spinach and coconut milk. Cover with lid for a few more minutes to allow the spinach to get warm (it will wilt). Serve over rice for a complete meal.

10. Boeufless Bourguignon (quicker) VEGAN

Boeuf Bourguignon is a traditional French recipe. According to the website *The French Traveler*:

This dish is prepared by braising the beef in a full-bodied, classic red (Burgundy) wine. It is then stewed with potatoes, carrots, onions, garlic, and well-seasoned (during the stewing process) with a bouquet garni, or a small satchel of thyme, parsley, and bay leaves.

Auguste Escoffier first published his version of this recipe in the early 20th century using whole pieces of beef. Later in the 20th century, chef Julia Child cut the beef into cubes for her version as published in Mastering the Art of French Cooking.

Neither Escoffier nor Julia Child would have appreciated my vegan version of Boeuf Bourguignon, but I am confident that you will. For my version, I substitute hearty mushrooms and Yukon potatoes for the beef and a full-bodied Pinot Noir for the Burgundy. I then add a little tomato paste and Sriracha sauce, which provides a unique burst of flavorful heat.

Ingredients:
4 tablespoons extra virgin olive oil (divided)
4 small Yukon Gold potatoes (cut in half and then into quarters)
10-ounce bag frozen pearl onions
1½ cups Pinot Noir (or any dry red wine)
1 pound sliced mushrooms

1 teaspoon garlic powder
½ teaspoon crushed rosemary (such as McCormick)
½ teaspoon ground thyme
14 ounces frozen sliced carrots (such as Birds Eye)
1 tablespoon tomato paste
1 teaspoons Sriracha sauce
1 tablespoon corn starch
1 teaspoon Better Than Bouillon Vegetable Base
4 cups vegetable broth
Salt and pepper to taste
Fresh parsley (chopped for garnish)

Directions:
Plug in and set slow cooker to high.

Place all ingredients except for parsley (garnish) in the slow cooker. Cook for 4 hours. Serve over fusilli pasta, garnish with parsley, and serve with a fresh loaf of crusty bread on the side for sopping up the Bourguignon sauce.

10. Boeufless Bourguignon (nutritious) VEGAN

Ingredients:
4 tablespoons extra virgin olive oil (divided)
4 small Yukon Gold potatoes (cut in half and then into quarters)
8 ounces pearl onions (peeled)
1½ cups Pinot Noir (or any dry red wine)
1 pound fresh Cremini mushrooms (stems removed –cut into quarters)
4 cloves garlic (minced)
1 teaspoon fresh rosemary (chopped fine)
1 teaspoon fresh thyme (chopped fine)
4 medium carrots (unpeeled, halved lengthwise and sliced into ¼ inch-thick pieces)
4 cups vegetable broth
1 teaspoon Better Than Bouillon Vegetable Base
1 tablespoon tomato paste
1 teaspoons Sriracha sauce
1 tablespoon corn starch
½ cup cold water
Salt and pepper to taste
Fresh parsley (chopped for garnish)
Cooked fusilli pasta

Directions:
Plug in and set slow cooker to high. Preheat oven to 400 degrees.

Place the potato quarters in a large baggie and add one tablespoon of oil. Shake to evenly coat potatoes with oil. Pour potatoes onto a large baking sheet and place in oven. Bake for 20 minutes or until a fork can barely pierce the potatoes. Remove from oven and set aside.

Heat a large heavy-bottomed pan over medium-high heat. Add one tablespoon of oil, then add the pearl onions and a pinch of salt, tossing to coat in the oil. Cook onions for 7-10 minutes, stirring occasionally, until golden brown. Deglaze pan with 1/4 cup wine and cook briefly to reduce wine and coat onions in the wine glaze. Transfer onions and glaze to the slow cooker.

Add one tablespoon of oil to the pan followed by the mushrooms and another pinch of salt. Cook, stirring occasionally until mushrooms are golden brown - about 5 minutes. Deglaze the pan with 1/4 cup wine, cooking briefly to reduce wine and coat mushrooms in the wine glaze. Transfer mushrooms and glaze to the slow cooker.

Turn the heat down to medium and add the remaining tablespoon of oil to the pan, followed by the garlic, rosemary, thyme, and carrots. Cook briefly until aromatic, then transfer to the slow cooker.

To the slow cooker, add the broth, bouillon, tomato paste, Sriracha, and remaining wine. That should be all of the ingredients except for the corn starch and water. Stir briefly and cook for 4 hours.

Mix corn starch in water until completely dissolved (no lumps). Add corn starch mixture to slow cooker and stir to combine. Cook uncovered for another 20 minutes. Taste and adjust for salt and pepper.

Serve over fusilli pasta, garnish with parsley, and serve with a fresh loaf of crusty bread on the side for sopping up the Bourguignon sauce.

11. Alphabet Soup (quicker)

As a kid, I couldn't wait for mom to make alphabet soup for Saturday lunch. I looked for pieces of macaroni to spell out my name and was usually disappointed that I couldn't find a "y" to complete my name. Then I was disappointed that the soup was no longer hot when I got around to eating it.

According to the website, triviahappy.com, alphabet soup has been around for quite a while:

> *Alphabet soup seems like an iconic piece of kitsch, canned by Campbell's and eaten around 1950s lunch tables. But the history of pasta-driven literacy is much longer than you'd expect. In fact, alphabet soup goes back 150 years, and people have been playing with it the entire time.*
>
> *In 1886, one paper published a tutorial about macaroni and included alphabet pasta in its list, as well as pasta in the shape of hearts, stars, and crowns. That entire decade, the ITALIAN MACARONI with the alphabetic shape was being sold across the country, but it was invented even earlier.*
>
> *Yes, alphabet soup was the hottest culinary innovation of...1867. Just after the Civil War, the Tri-Weekly Standard in Raleigh first reported on a new fun type of food. The short item marveled:*

The latest culinary novelty is alphabetical soup. Instead of the usual cylindric and star shaped morsels of macaroni which have hitherto given body to our broth, the letters of the alphabet have been substituted. These letters of paste preserve their forms in passing through the pot.

So now you know the history of alphabet soup. Make my version and enjoy trying to spell out your name but be sure to take a bite along the way. It's much better while still hot!

Ingredients:
1 vegetable bouillon cube
28-ounce can stewed tomatoes (with liquid)
1 cup sliced carrots (such as Birds Eye)
1/3 cup dried celery flakes (such as McCormick)
1/2 cup ready chopped onions (such as Birds Eye)
1 cup sliced fresh mushrooms
1 tablespoon dried basil
1 teaspoon salt
¼ teaspoon pepper
5 cups vegetable broth
2 cups alphabet pasta (such as Davinci)
Parmesan cheese (grated for garnish)

Directions:
Plug in and set slow cooker to low.

Add all the ingredients to the slow cooker except for the pasta and cheese. Cover and cook for 7 hours. Taste and adjust for salt, if necessary.

Add pasta and stir. Turn heat setting to high and cook for 20-30 minutes or until pasta is done. To serve, ladle soup into bowls and sprinkle cheese on top. I like to bring extra cheese to the table in case I need more for my soup.

11. Alphabet Soup (nutritious)

Ingredients:
2 teaspoons Better Than Bouillon Vegetable Base
28-ounce can stewed tomatoes (with liquid)
1 cup fresh carrots (sliced)
1 cup fresh celery (sliced)
1/2 cup yellow onion (chopped)
1 cup fresh cremini mushrooms (sliced)
¼ cup fresh basil (chopped)
1 teaspoon salt
¼ teaspoon cracked black pepper
5 cups vegetable broth
2 cups alphabet pasta (such as Davinci)
Parmesan cheese (grated for garnish)

Directions:
Plug in and set slow cooker to low.

Add all the ingredients to the slow cooker except for the pasta and cheese. Cover and cook for 7 hours.

Add pasta and stir. Turn heat setting to high and cook for 20-30 minutes or until pasta is done. To serve, ladle soup into bowls and sprinkle cheese on top. I like to bring extra cheese to the table in case I need more for my soup.

12. Butternut Squash Soup (quicker) *VEGAN*

What is the difference between soup and stew? Stews are thicker and chunkier and could, if you want, be described as really thick soups. Stews often are thickened with potatoes and almost always served hot. The liquid in a stew is minimal to the point of being more of a gravy than a broth. In reality, a stew is usually considered a main dish and soup the first course.

Make this vegan soup first thing in the morning, and it will be thick, chunky and ready for dinner that night. Squeezing a little lemon juice into it just before eating gives this soup a unique flavor that I think you will like.

Ingredients
2 tablespoons extra-virgin olive oil
1 tablespoon onion powder
½ teaspoon garlic powder
2 tablespoons tomato paste
¼ teaspoon red pepper flakes
2 15-ounce cans chickpeas (including liquid)
10 ounces frozen cubed butternut squash (such as Earthbound Farm)
1 teaspoon salt
5 cups vegetable broth
10 ounces frozen spinach leaves (such as Birds Eye)
Lemon wedges (to squeeze on the soup when served)

Directions:
Plug in and set slow cooker to high.

Add first nine ingredients (oil through broth) to the slow cooker. Gently stir, cover, and cook for 3 hours.

Before serving, lift the lid and stir in the spinach leaves. Cover and continue cooking 15 more minutes more on high. Spoon the soups into bowls and serve with a plate of lemon wedges on the side.

12. Butternut Squash Soup (nutritious) VEGAN

Ingredients:
1 pound uncooked butternut squash
3 tablespoons extra-virgin olive oil
1 medium onion (sliced thin)
2 cloves garlic (minced)
2 tablespoons tomato paste
¼ teaspoon red pepper flakes
1 cup dried chickpeas
1 teaspoon salt
2 quarts vegetable broth
1 tablespoon Better than Bouillon Vegetable Base
6 to 8 ounces fresh baby spinach leaves
Lemon wedges (to squeeze on the soup when served)

Directions:
Plug in and set slow cooker to high.

Cut squash in half and scoop out seeds. Peel squash and cut into 1½ inch cubes. Set aside.

Heat the olive oil in a large pan over medium-high heat. Add the onion and garlic and cook until soft - about 4 minutes. Stir in the tomato paste and red pepper flakes and cook 1 minute more. Stir in ½ cup broth and scrape the bottom to deglaze the pan. Transfer the contents to a slow cooker.

Add the chickpeas, squash, salt, broth, and bouillon to the slow cooker. Gently stir, cover, and cook for 4 hours.

Before serving, lift the lid and stir in the spinach leaves. Cover and continue cooking 10 more minutes more on high. Spoon the soup into bowls and serve with a plate of lemon wedges on the side.

13. Chik'n Tikka Masala (quicker) VEGAN

Tikka is the Punjabi word for an Indian dish of small pieces of meat or vegetables marinated in a spice mixture. Masala is an Urdu word for any of a number of spice mixtures ground into a paste or powder for use in Indian cooking. When you put them together, you get a rich, creamy, and very flavorful curry with small pieces of meat or vegetables. My version, of course, does not have meat.

Traditional tikka masala sauce is made with heavy cream. I substitute coconut milk to keep this vegan. If you eat dairy products, I recommend using heavy cream. For a complete meal, serve over steamed rice.

Ingredients:
1 package Quorn Vegan Chik'n Tenders (thawed)
4 teaspoons onion powder
½ teaspoon garlic powder
½ teaspoon ground ginger
2 tablespoons tomato paste
2 tablespoons garam masala
2 teaspoons paprika
2 teaspoons salt
28-ounce can fire roasted tomatoes (diced)
½ cup water
¾ cup unsweetened coconut milk
Fresh cilantro (chopped for garnish)

Directions:
Plug in and set slow cooker to low.

Add first 11 ingredients (Quorn through coconut milk) to slow cooker. Cover the slow cooker and cook for 4 hours. Taste and add more garam masala to taste. Sprinkle with cilantro and serve while still hot.

Note: This makes enough for 2 to 3 hungry adults. It may easily be doubled to feed more.

13. Chik'n Tikka Masala (nutritious) VEGAN

Ingredients:
1 large onion (diced)
3 cloves garlic (minced)
1 teaspoon extra virgin olive oil
1-inch piece whole ginger (peeled and grated)
2 tablespoons tomato paste
2 tablespoons garam masala
2 teaspoons ground Aleppo pepper (or substitute paprika)
2 teaspoons salt
1 package Quorn Vegan Chik'n Tenders (thawed)
28-ounce can fire roasted tomatoes (diced)
¾ cup unsweetened coconut milk
½ cup water
4 cups steamed rice
Fresh cilantro (chopped for garnish)

Directions:
Plug in and set slow cooker to low.

Sauté the onions and garlic in the olive oil over medium-high heat until softened –about 5 minutes. Stir in the ginger, tomato paste, and spices (garam masala through salt) until fragrant.

Transfer the onion mixture to the slow cooker. Add the Quorn, diced tomatoes, water, and coconut milk. Cover the slow cooker and cook for 4 hours. Taste and add more garam masala to taste. To serve, spoon over steamed rice and sprinkle with cilantro.

Note: This makes enough for 2 to 3 hungry adults. It may easily be doubled to feed more.

14. Lentil Stew with Sausage (quicker)

Lentils are low in calories, high in fiber, high in protein and have zero trans fats. This basic lentil recipe is simple and easy to prepare. Just put all the ingredients into a slow cooker and the chow down 4 hours later. The vegetarian sausage adds depth and texture to a hearty stew. It's especially good on a cold winter night.

Ingredients:
1½ cups lentils (black lentils are good, but any lentils will do)
1 package Lightlife Smart Sausages Italian Style (cut into ½-inch pieces)
2 cups frozen sweet corn kernels
¼ cup celery flakes
3 carrots (cut into one-inch pieces)
1 tablespoon onion powder
15-ounce diced tomatoes (including liquid)
½ teaspoon garlic powder
Salt to taste
1 vegetable bouillon cube
4 cups vegetable broth

Directions:
Plug in and set slow cooker to high.

Rinse the lentils and cull out small stones and debris. Add the lentils and the other ingredients to the crock-pot. Cook for 4 hours. Before serving, taste and adjust for more salt if necessary. Serve with slices of fresh French bread.

14. Lentil Stew with Sausage (nutritious)

Ingredients:
1½ cups lentils (black lentils are good but any lentils will do)
1 package Lightlife Smart Sausages Italian Style (cut into ½-inch pieces)
2 cups sweet corn kernels
3 stalks celery (thinly sliced)
3 carrots (cut into one-inch pieces)
1 medium onion (chopped)
15-ounce can diced tomatoes (including liquid)
2 cloves garlic (minced)
1 tablespoon Better Than Bouillon (vegetable base)
4 cups vegetable broth

Directions:
Plug in and set slow cooker to high.

Rinse the lentils and cull out small stones and debris. Add the lentils and all other ingredients to the crock-pot. Cook for 4 hours.

This makes a meal all by itself but is even better and more nutritious when accompanied by rice.

15. Mulligatawny Soup (quicker) VEGAN

Mulligatawny is the Anglicized version of the Tamil words for "pepper water" or "pepper broth." It became popular with employees of the East India Company during colonial times in India. When they returned home, they brought the recipe back with them to England.

Mulligatawny was originally a creamy curried soup made with peppers (hence the name). Over time it has gone through many variations. It is usually based on a chicken stock and curry, with cream, pieces of chicken, onion, celery, apples, and almonds. Today's American version bears little resemblance to the original.

My version is vegan, gluten-free and makes a whole bunch of soup. Share some with your friends and neighbors!

Ingredients:
1 tablespoon extra-virgin olive oil
1½ teaspoons garlic powder
½ teaspoon dried ginger
2 teaspoons mild curry powder
1 teaspoon turmeric
1/2 teaspoon cayenne pepper
1 tablespoon onion powder
12 baby or petite cut carrots (such as Bolthouse Farms)
1 cup frozen cauliflower florets (such as Birds Eye)
½ cup diced dried apples (such as Bob's Red Mill)

1 ½ cup frozen sweet potato chunks (such as Archer Farms)
10 ounces angel hair shredded cabbage (such as Dole)
1 quart water (or vegetable broth)
2 cups vegetable juice (such as V-8)
15-ounce can chickpeas (drained)
15-ounce can coconut milk (stir it thoroughly)
1 tablespoon lime juice

Directions:
Plug in and set slow cooker to high.

Combine all of the ingredients in a slow cooker except the coconut milk and lime juice. Cover and cook for 3 hours. Add the coconut milk and lime juice and mix well. Cover and continue to heat for another 15 minutes.

Note: This makes 6 quarts of soup so you will need a 6-quart slow cooker for this recipe. If you prefer a smoother texture, remove half of the soup to a blender. Puree and add back to the chunky original. Stir thoroughly before serving.

15. Mulligatawny Soup (nutritious) *VEGAN*

Ingredients:
1 tablespoon extra-virgin olive oil
4 cloves garlic (minced)
1 inch fresh ginger (grated)
2 teaspoons mild curry powder
1 teaspoon turmeric
1/2 teaspoon cayenne pepper
1 medium red onion (diced)
4 medium carrots (scrubbed and diced - not peeled)
1 cup fresh cauliflower florets (chopped)
2 large Granny Smith apples (peeled, cored and diced)
1 medium sweet potato (peeled and diced)
2 heaping cups thinly shredded cabbage
1 quart water (or vegetable broth)
2 cups vegetable juice (such as V-8)
15-ounce can chickpeas (drained)
15-ounce can coconut milk (stir it thoroughly)
1 tablespoon fresh lime juice
1 apple of your choice (peeled and shredded)

Directions:
Plug in and set slow cooker to high.

Combine the first 15 ingredients (oil thru chickpeas) in slow cooker. Cover and cook for 3 hours. Add the coconut milk and lime juice and mix well. Cover and continue to heat for another 15 minutes.

To serve, garnish with shredded apple and serve while still hot.

Note: This makes 6 quarts of soup so you will need a 6-quart slow cooker for this recipe. If you prefer a smoother texture, remove half of the soup to a blender. Puree and add back to the chunky original. Stir thoroughly before serving.

16. Risotto with Barley (quicker)

Who'd a thought you could make a tasty and easy risotto with barley?

Barley is a versatile cereal grain with a rich nutlike flavor and an appealing chewy, pasta-like consistency. It is the perfect substitute for Arborio rice in risotto. It is touted as one of the world's healthiest foods having an abundance of manganese, magnesium, selenium, copper, chromium, Vitamins B1 and B3, and fiber.*

Serve with a side of salad, and you have a complete meal!

Ingredients:
5 tablespoons butter
¼ teaspoon onion powder
1½ cups pearl barley
16 ounces sliced mushrooms
1 teaspoon salt
½ teaspoon freshly ground pepper
2 tablespoons dry white wine
4 cups vegetable broth
2 teaspoons dried parsley flakes
1 teaspoon dried sage
¾ cup finely grated Parmesan cheese (divided)

Directions:
Plug in and set slow cooker to low.

Add all ingredients to the slow cooker except the cheese. Cook for 3 hours. If the barley is not tender after 3 hours, replace the cover, set heat to high, and set the timer for another 30 minutes. Stir in ½ cup of the cheese.

Serve family-style by transfer to a large serving bowl and garnished with the remaining ¼ cup cheese. Bring to the table while still hot.

Barley has gluten proteins so if you have celiac disease it is not a safe grain for you. Try substituting sorghum grain instead.

16. Risotto with Barley (nutritious)

Ingredients:
5 tablespoons unsalted butter (divided)
2 tablespoons extra-virgin olive oil (divided)
½ cup shallots (chopped fine)
1½ cups pearl barley
1½ teaspoons salt
½ teaspoon freshly ground pepper
¼ cup dry white wine
16 ounces Cremini mushrooms, (sliced thin)
4 cups vegetable broth
2 teaspoons Better Than Bouillon Vegetable Base
2 tablespoons fresh parsley (chopped)
1 tablespoon fresh sage (chopped)
¾ cup finely grated Parmigiano-Reggiano

Directions:
Plug in and set slow cooker to low.

Heat 1 tablespoon of the butter and one tablespoon of the oil in a large pan over medium-high heat. Add the shallots and cook, while stirring, until tender –about 2 minutes. Add the barley, salt, and pepper and cook for 1 minute more. Pour in wine and cook, stirring, until the wine is mostly evaporated –about 3 minutes. Transfer this mixture to a slow cooker and cover.

Using the same large pan on medium-high heat, add two tablespoons of the butter and the remaining one tablespoon oil. Add the mushrooms and cook until lightly browned and wilted –about 5 minutes.

Add the mushrooms, broth, and bouillon to the slow cooker. Stir gently to combine. Cook for 3 hours. If the barley is not tender after 3 hours, replace the cover, set heat to high, and set the timer for another 30 minutes.

Stir in the parsley, sage, ½ cup of the cheese and the remaining 2 tablespoons butter. Transfer to a large serving bowl and garnish with the remaining ¼ cup cheese. Bring to the table while still hot.

Barley has gluten proteins so if you have celiac disease it is not a safe grain for you. Try substituting sorghum grain instead.

17. Southwest Vegetarian Stew (quicker)

Remembering a satisfying bowl of southwest vegetarian stew I ordered off the menu at a diner in Roswell, New Mexico, I created this recipe for the slow cooker. This may sound similar to my Savory Vegetarian Stew but trust me, it isn't. The ingredients and the flavors it brings are considerably different.

Ingredients:
15-ounce can black beans (drained and rinsed)
15-ounce can fire roasted tomatoes (diced)
15-ounce can creamed corn
15-ounce can Southwest Corn with Peppers (such as Del Monte)
1 cup ready chopped onions (such as Birds Eye)
5 tablespoons dried bell pepper flakes (such as Cain's)
½ teaspoon garlic powder
1 teaspoon chili powder
½ teaspoon cumin
3½ cups low-sodium vegetable broth
Fresh ground black pepper to taste
1/3 cup instant mashed potato flakes
¼ cup sour cream (garnish)
½ cup tri-color tortilla strips (garnish)

Directions:
Plug in and set slow cooker to high.

Add first 11 ingredients (black beans to black pepper) to slow cooker. Cover and cook for 3½ hours. Mix corn starch with cold water. Stir corn starch mixture into stew and allow to cook for 15 minutes more uncovered.

To serve, spoon into bowls and drizzle a little sour cream on top. Garnish with a few tortilla strips. Serve while piping hot from the slow cooker.

17. Southwest Vegetarian Stew (nutritious)

Ingredients:
3½ cups vegetable broth
15-ounce can black beans (drained and rinsed)
15-ounce can fire roasted tomatoes (diced)
15-ounce can creamed corn
3 ears fresh corn (remove husk/silk and trim off kernels)
1 cup red onion (diced)
1 cup bell pepper (diced)
2 cloves garlic (peeled and minced)
1 teaspoon chili powder
½ teaspoon cumin
Fresh ground black pepper to taste
1 tablespoon corn starch
½ cup cold water
¼ cup sour cream (garnish)
8 pickled jalapeño nacho slices (garnish)
½ cup tri-color tortilla strips (garnish)

Directions:
Plug in and set slow cooker to high.

Add first 11 ingredients (broth to black pepper) to slow cooker. Cover and cook for 3½ hours. Mix corn starch with cold water. Stir corn starch mixture into stew and allow to cook for 15 minutes more uncovered.

To serve, spoon into bowls, drizzle a little sour cream on top, and lay a couple of jalapeño slices on top of that. Garnish with a few tortilla strips and serve while piping hot from the slow cooker.

18. Navy Bean Soup (quicker) *VEGAN*

The navy bean got its current popular name because it was a staple food of the United States Navy in the early 20th century. They are a mild, pea-sized bean that is white.

Like other common beans, navy beans are one of 13,000 species of the family of legumes, or plants that produce edible pods. Combined with whole grains such as rice, navy beans provide a virtually fat-free high-quality protein.

Ingredients:
2 15-ounce cans navy beans –drained (such as Bush's)
1 tablespoon onion powder
1 teaspoon garlic powder
1 teaspoon dried dill
1 tablespoon dried parsley flakes
2 15-ounce cans whole new potatoes –cut in half (such as Del Monte)
14 ounces frozen sliced carrots (such as Birds Eye)
1 cup sun-dried tomatoes (chopped)
2 teaspoons salt
¼ teaspoon pepper
5 cups vegetable broth

Directions:
Plug in and set slow cooker to high.

Place all ingredients in slow cooker. Cook for 3 hours. Before serving, adjust for salt adding more if necessary. Serve with a side of rice for a complete meal.

18. Navy Bean Soup (nutritious) *VEGAN*

Ingredients:
1 pound dry navy beans (rinsed)
1 medium onion (diced)
1 tablespoon fresh dill (chopped)
4 tablespoon fresh parsley (chopped)
4 cloves garlic (minced)
2 medium russet potatoes (peeled and diced)
4 large carrots (scrubbed and cut into ¼-inch slices)
1 cup sun-dried tomatoes (chopped)
2 teaspoons salt
¼ teaspoon fresh ground black pepper
2 quarts vegetable broth

Directions:
Plug in and set slow cooker to high.

Place all ingredients in slow cooker. Cook for 5 hours. Before serving, adjust for salt adding more if necessary. Serve with a side of rice for a complete meal.

19. Quinoa and Chik'n Enchiladas (quicker)

When my young 12-year old friend saw me preparing this for our family and his, he asked, *How the heck can you make enchiladas in a slow cooker? That just doesn't sound right.*

I like that all of the ingredients in the slow cooker come together for a taste that is amazingly good and, unlike traditional enchiladas, is a lot easier to make. When my friend tasted this slow cooker enchilada, he exclaimed, *Amazing! You can make this for mom and me anytime.*

Ingredients:
2 packages Quorn Vegan Chik'n Tenders
1½ cups uncooked quinoa (such as Bob's Red Mill)
15-ounce can black beans (drained and rinsed)
2 cups frozen corn (such as Birds Eye)
1 cup ready chopped onions (such as Birds Eye)
15-ounce can diced fire roasted tomatoes
½ teaspoon garlic powder
¼ cup nacho-sliced pickled jalapeno peppers
1½ cups water
10-ounce can red enchilada sauce (such as Old El Paso)
2 tablespoons chili powder
1 tablespoon cumin
2 teaspoons ground coriander
2 cups shredded Mexican blend cheese (divided)
3 green onions (chopped for garnish)
¼ cup fresh cilantro (chopped for garnish)

Directions:
Plug in and set slow cooker to high.

Add the first 13 ingredients (Quorn through coriander) to the slow cooker. Stir to combine. Cover and cook for 3 hours.

Remove the lid and stir everything again. Taste and adjust for salt if necessary. Stir in 1 cup of the cheese and transfer to individual bowls. To serve, evenly sprinkle the balance of cheese on top of each bowl. Top with green onions and cilantro and serve with warm corn tortillas on the side.

19. Quinoa and Chik'n Enchiladas (nutritious)

Ingredients:
2 packages Quorn Vegan Chik'n Tenders
1½ cups uncooked quinoa (such as Bob's Red Mill)
15-ounce can black beans (drained and rinsed)
2 cobs of fresh corn (shuck and slice off corn)
15-ounce can diced fire roasted tomatoes
2 cloves garlic (minced)
1 medium white onion (chopped)
2 jalapeno peppers (seeded and chopped)
1½ cup water
10-ounce can red enchilada sauce (such as Old El Paso)
2 tablespoons chili powder
1 tablespoon cumin
2 teaspoons ground coriander
Salt to taste
1 cup shredded Mexican blend cheese (divided)
3 green onions (chopped for garnish)
¼ cup fresh cilantro (chopped for garnish)

Directions:
Plug in and set slow cooker to high.

Add the first 13 ingredients (Quorn through coriander) to the slow cooker. Stir to combine. Cover and cook for 3 hours.

Remove the lid and stir everything again. Taste and adjust for salt if necessary. Stir in 1 cup of the cheese and transfer to individual bowls. To serve, evenly sprinkle the balance of cheese on top of each bowl. Top with green onions and cilantro and serve with warm corn tortillas on the side.

20. Apple Butter

When Robin and I married, and set up our kitchen, one of the first things we made together was apple butter. We'd make twice as much as we could eat so we could share with our family and friends.

This is our original recipe, tweaked slightly for the slow cooker. It is as good today as it was 40 years ago.

Ingredients:
6 pounds apples (peeled, cored and sliced)
1 cup sugar
1 cup light brown sugar (packed light)
1 tablespoon cinnamon
½ teaspoon ground nutmeg
¼ teaspoon ground cloves
¼ teaspoon salt
1 tablespoon vanilla extract

Directions:
Plug in and set slow cooker to low.

Place the apples in a slow cooker. In a medium bowl, combine sugars, cinnamon, nutmeg, cloves, and salt. Pour the mixture over the apples and mix well.

Cook for 10 hours, stirring occasionally, until the mixture is thickened and dark brown. Uncover, stir in vanilla and continue cooking uncovered on low for another hour. Use an immersion blender to puree until the apples are buttery smooth.

Spoon the mixture into sterile containers, cover, and refrigerate for up to ten days. Serve on bread, muffins, peanut and butter sandwiches, or just eat it with a spoon.

Note: I use apples from our tree in the front yard. Have no idea what type they are. Adjust sugar according to your apples and preferences. This makes about seven half-pints of goodness.

21. Bananas Foster

According to WhatsCookingAmerica.net:

In the 1950's, New Orleans was the major port of entry for bananas shipped from Central and South America. In 1951, Owen Edward Brennan challenged his talented chef, Paul Blang to include bananas in a new culinary creation.

The scrumptious dessert was named for Richard Foster, who, as chairman, served with Owen on the New Orleans Crime Commission, a civic effort to clean up the French Quarter. Richard Foster, owner of the Foster Awning Company, was a frequent customer of Brennan's and a very good friend of Owen.

Little did anyone realize that Bananas Foster would become an international favorite and is the most requested item on the restaurant's menu. Thirty-five thousand pounds of bananas are flamed each year at Brennan's in the preparation of its world-famous dessert.

Here's my version of Bananas Foster –slow cooker style!

Ingredients:
1 cup dark brown sugar
1 stick butter (cut into small pieces)
½ teaspoon cinnamon
1 teaspoon vanilla
¼ cup dark rum

¼ cup water
4 bananas (cut into 2" pieces)
Vanilla ice cream or gelato (optional)

Directions:
Plug in and set slow cooker to high. Add in everything except bananas. Mix well. Add in bananas. Gently toss with your fingers so bananas don't get smashed.

Cook on high for 2½ hours. Uncover and gently mix once more. Spoon over your favorite vanilla ice cream or gelato and serve with a smile. It's gonna taste sooooo good.

Note: Choose bananas that are yellow, not green. They should not have black pots of ripeness on the skin. You don't want super ripe bananas for this recipe. And sorry, no flambé! The alcohol in the rum will have evaporated during the cooking process.

22. Dulce de Leche

How do you pronounce this culinary delight, you ask? Some pronounce it "doolchay day laychay" but that would be wrong. It is correctly pronounced "doolsā de leCHā."

Dulce is the Spanish language word for sweet. Leche is the word for milk. To call it "sweet milk" in English, however, does not do it justice. Think creamy, thick caramel goodness because that's what it is.

It is made from whole cow's milk and at times, goat's milk or coconut milk. My version is made from sweetened condensed cow's milk and is tasty and quick to make.

So, once it is made, *how do I enjoy this wonderfully easy-to-make dessert?* I eat it straight from the slow cooker. Just one teaspoon is enough to satisfy my sweet craving for 24 hours and more. I also spread it between two graham crackers and munch down (better than s'mores in my opinion). You may want to spoon it over ice cream or use as a filling for cakes or cookies.

I have a fantastic recipe for Dulce de Leche Chocolate Chip Cookies...but that's another recipe for another time!

Ingredients:
2 14-ounce cans sweetened condensed milk

water
4 clean half-pint jars (with lids)

Directions:
Plug in and set slow cooker to low.

Divide the sweetened condensed milk among the 4 jars. Seal the jars with clean lids and rings and place in the slow cooker. Making sure the jars do not touch.

Fill the crockpot with water until water is about two inches above the tops of the jars. Cover and cook for nine hours.

When finished cooking, carefully remove the jars and place them on your kitchen counter to cool. Once cool, they should keep in the refrigerator for three weeks or more —although they'll probably be consumed way before that.

Index of Recipes by Title

Alphabet Soup (11)
Apple Butter (20)
Bananas Foster (21)
Beefless Stew with Sofrito (3)
Boeufless Bourguignon (10)
Butternut Squash Stew (12)
Chik'n Tikka Masala (13)
Chili Verde (7)
Curried Vegetable and Chickpea Stew (9)
Dulce de Leche (22)
Hearty Chili Bean Soup (2)
Hearty Sorghum Soup (8)
Lentil Stew with Sausage (14)
Minestrone Soup (4)
Mulligatawny Soup (15)
Navy Bean Soup (18)
Quinoa and Chik'n Enchilada Casseroale (19)
Risotto with Barley (16)
Savory Vegetarian Stew (1)
Southwest Vegetarian Stew (17)
Spinach, Bean, and Sausage Soup (6)
Taste of Morocco (5)

Index of Ingredients by Recipe

A
alphabet pasta, 11
apples, 15, 20
apricots, 5

B
bananas, 21
barley, 16
basil, 1, 2, 4, 11
bay leaves, 1, 4, 6, 8
bell pepper, 2, 17
black beans, 17, 19
bouillon, 2, 4, 10, 11, 14
brown sugar, 20, 21
butter, 16, 21
butternut squash, 12

C
cabbage, 15
cannellini beans, 4, 6
carrots, 1, 2, 4, 5, 8, 10, 11, 14, 15, 18
cauliflower, 9, 15
cayenne pepper, 9, 15
celery, 4, 6, 8, 11, 14
chickpeas, 5, 9, 12, 15
chili powder, 2, 7, 17, 19
cilantro, 5, 7, 13, 19
cinnamon, 5, 20, 21
cloves, 1, 20
coconut milk, 9, 13, 15
coriander, 19
corn, 14, 19
corn starch, 1, 10
creamed corn, 1
cumin, 2, 5, 7, 17, 19
curry powder, 9, 15

D
dill, 18

E
enchilada sauce, 7, 19

G
garam masala, 13
Gardein Beefless Tips, 3
garlic, 1, 2, 3, 4, 5, 6, 7, 8, 9, 10, 12, 13, 14, 15, 17, 18, 19
ginger, 9, 13, 15
green beans, 4
green peppers, 9

I
ice cream, 21

J
jalapeno peppers, 19

K
kidney beans, 4

L
lemon, 12
lentils, 14
lime juice, 2, 15

M
Mexican blend cheese, 19
mint, 5
mushrooms, 8, 10, 11, 16

N
navy beans, 18
nutmeg, 20

O
olive oil, 5, 6, 8, 9, 10, 12, 15
olives, 3
onion powder, 1, 2, 4, 5, 12, 13, 14, 15, 16, 18
onions, 3, 6, 7, 8, 9, 10, 11, 17, 19
orange rind, 1
oregano, 2, 4, 6

P
potatoes, 9
paprika, 5, 13
Parmesan cheese, 11, 16
parsley, 4, 10, 16, 18
pinto beans, 2
potato flakes, 17
potatoes, 1, 2, 3, 10, 18

Q
quinoa, 19
Quorn Vegan Chik'n Tenders, 7, 13, 19

R
raisins, 5
red pepper flakes, 12
Romano cheese, 8
rosemary, 10
rum, 21

S
sage, 1, 16
sausage, 6, 14
sofrito, 3
sorghum, 8
sour cream, 8, 17
spinach, 4, 6, 9, 12
Sriracha sauce, 10
sweet potato, 15
sweetened condensed milk, 22

T
thyme, 4, 8, 10
tofu, 1, 5
tomato paste, 10, 12, 13
tomatoes, 2, 3, 4, 7, 9, 11, 13, 14, 17, 18, 19

tortilla strips, 17
turmeric, 15

V
vanilla, 20, 21
vegetable broth, 1, 4, 5, 6, 8, 9, 10, 11, 12, 14, 15, 16, 17, 18
vegetable juice, 15

W
wine, 1, 10, 16

Z
zucchini, 4

About the Author

My wife, Robin, and I live in Ojai, California with our dog Willow. Robin and Willow are not vegetarians.

I have been a vegetarian since August 1975 and eat local and organic grain, fresh fruit, and vegetables as much as possible. I enjoy cooking for friends and family using ingredients from backyard vegetable and herb gardens. I am known locally as the "Healthy Chef." My food is often called vegetarian comfort food and real food for real people. My recipe column, Chef Randy, is syndicated in California newspapers. Contact me through my website at Valley-Vegetarian.com.

Made in the USA
San Bernardino, CA
10 October 2018